THE POWER

OF

METHODS

The Right Decision In
Getting To Your Goals

SERVAAS STEENKAMP

Jirah Pro Consultants (Pty) Ltd.
Copyright © SERVAAS 2018

The Power of Methods

THE POWER OF METHODS
Copyright © 2018 by Servaas Steenkamp

All rights reserved. No part of this publication may be reproduced,
distributed, or transmitted in any form or by any means, including
photocopying, recording, or any other electronic or mechanical methods,
without the prior written permission of the publisher, except in the case of
brief quotations embodied in critical reviews and certain other
noncommercial uses permitted by copyright law. For permission requests,
email the publisher, at the address below:
servaas@jirahproconsultants.co.za

Jirah Pro Consultants (Pty) Ltd. 20 Minnaar street, Forest Hill,
Johannesburg, 2190, First Edition
www.jirahproconsultants.co.za

ISBN-10:1725512823
ISBN-13:978-1725512825

The Power of Methods

What Your About To Master

The Power of Methods is a business system that was designed to help any business man or woman in the world. In fact, it can be used by anyone who has a goal in mind to quickly get them on track to achieving them. With this information in this book, you can go from earning nothing, to building a profitable business and generate millions of dollars by simply meeting your own goals. It is extremely powerful in the sense of the skill sets you are about to learn. It does not matter if you think you can not achieve your dream, or that you have even considered achieving your dream. If you follow these principles laid out in this book, you will be in the race to your success and possibly your purpose in life. You don't need experience to be able to apply these principles. All that matters is the attitude at which you desire your success in life, in your

The Power of Methods

business and in your goals. If you desire financial freedom and success in all areas of your goals, this book is for you. Author Servaas Steenkamp is about to rock your world and take you on a life changing journey, starting with nothing more than a desire to succeed. He had no experience, some technical knowledge and absolutely no idea what he was doing. He became addicted to the idea of changing one's path through Methods and so this book was born. The Power of Methods is a life long dedication of Servaas Steenkamp's life, time and money. He is obsessed with living a life of passion and creating a life worth living with. In this first edition of The Power of Methods you will see that Servaas Steenkamp is truly interested in helping people like you succeed. He not only made sure the content is rich and up to date but offers a once in a life time opportunity to all who read this book. To find out that opportunity you will have to finish reading this book. If you have dreamed of having more for yourself, business and in life, The Power of Methods is exactly the system that will get you there.

The Power of Methods

About The Author

Servaas Steenkamp started his business in the year 2014 and had no clue what he actually wanted to do. He had absolutely no experience in business at all. He didn't even know how to register his business. He stumbled upon a world full of information and confusion. Every place he looked left him with more questions rather than answers. After a year and a half of struggling to find answers, he was about to give in to his desire. The desire to give up trying to reach his goals, then finally he came to place where he understood the secret code of achieving goals. It was a so called epiphany. The key to achieving any goal has to have a means to it. What is the means to which any goal is achieved is determined through some external factors that will be discussed in this book. He started elaborating on this epiphany and designing the course you are about to go through. This course helped our author to go from a low paying job to a

The Power of Methods

higher paying job. From earning nothing with the business to making thousands of dollars with the business. The sky is the limit. This book helped Servaas Steenkamp and he wanted to share this epiphany with you. His journey was not easy and he experienced many ups and downs. He nearly went bankrupt mastering what he is about to teach you. Since he started teaching this system to small business all over South-Africa, Servaas Steenkamp has helped countless startups and well established business' achieve their own goals. They seemed to have an invisible wall stopping them from achieving their goals, but through this system our author and his team smashed those barriers. Servaas Steenkamp is a well spoken motivational entrepreneur and business coach today. He has influenced many people over the years to achieve more than they thought possible. During his career, Servaas Steenkamp has made millions in revenue using this simple and easy to follow system, that is now presented to you as The Power of Methods. He has made it his personal mission to spread The Power and to enable people, like yourself, and business' to achieving their God given dream. Are your ready to take the right steps in the right direction and join Servaas Steenkamp on his journey? Then let's get into it and read The Power of Methods.

The Power of Methods

Dedication

I dedicate this book to everyone who has supported and inspired me. To my Lord And Saviour Jesus Christ. My parents, my wife, my sister, brother and my two wonderful Pastors Gavin and Pastor Vicky Enslin. You provide me the endless support I need to go conquer the day. You understand my outrageous dreams and you push me forward as I hunt them down! Thank you. To my friends. When life gets tough, you are always there to cheer me up. Even when I disappear mentally at times as I am immersed in something, when I come back, you are right there and ready to receive me. Thank you for being such awesome friends. I could never do it without you guys. To my team. Where to start? None of my outrageous dreams would ever have come true if I did not have your support and hard-work. I am honestly in awe of your talents, dedication & work ethic. Thank you so much for supporting me no matter how

The Power of Methods

hard it gets! You guys rock! This book, I dedicate to all of you! - Servaas Steenkamp

The Power of Methods

The First Chapter
    The First Chapter
    1. A Dream Forgotten
    2. My Life Changing Decision
    3. The Epiphany Moment
    4. The Birth of The Power of Methods

The First Hurdle
    The First Hurdle
    1. Before You Start
    2. The M In Methods
    3. The E In Methods
    4. The T In Methods
    5. The H In Methods
    6. The O In Methods
    7. The D In Methods
    8. The S In Methods
    9. The Closing Arrangements

What is TALK?
    What is TALK?
    1. The TALK Methodology
    2. Building Block or Sandcastles
    3. Putting Action To Sand

I'm an IDIOT, really?
    I'm an IDIOT, really?
    1. The IDIOT Methodology
    2. The I in IDIOT

The Power of Methods

    3. The D in IDIOT
    4. The Second I in IDIOT
    5. The O in IDIOT
    6. The T in IDIOT

Your Crash Course to the Methods Methodology

    Your Crash Course to the Methods Methodology
    1. The Methods Methodology

The Second Hurdle

    The Second Hurdle
    1. What is NURTURE Leadership?
    2. The N in Nurture
    3. The U in Nurture
    4. The R in Nurture
    5. The T in Nurture
    6. The Second U in Nurture
    7. The Second R in Nurture
    8. The E in Nurture

What is Your PLAN?

    What Is Your PLAN?
    1. What Is Your PLAN?
    2. The P in Plan
    3. The L in Plan
    4. The A in Plan
    5. The N in Plan
    6. Closing Arrangements

What does it mean to be HUMAN?

    What Does It Mean To Be HUMAN?
    1. What Does It Mean To Be HUMAN?
    2. The H in Human
    3. The U in Human
    4. The M in Human

The Power of Methods

5. The A in Human
6. The N in Human

The Power of Methods

Foreword

"The world has a message that does not cater for people like me. I cannot consume their negative message anymore. I decided to write this book for the sole purpose because the message helped me. My desire is to bless all of you who are reading this book. This book took me a lot of time to write. I wish I could say that I'm this great author with all the right words, but as you will see in this book, I am a very simple writer. I merely wanted this content to be reached by people like you and me. We have had a vision, we have had a dream, but struggled to get it manifested into the real world. We are dreamers and leaders. We are the generation of people that will change this world for the better. It's not like we don't have anything better to do with our time, but we choose to increase our knowledge in hope that all this head-space will be occupied with the very thing that will bring our dreams to light. I don't claim to be the

The Power of Methods

smartest man alive, I wish though, but what I do believe is this: this book will change the way you tackle challenges in your business and in your life. I don't just write this to the business people, but equally so to those who have a dream of learning a new skill. To those who dream that there is something more. To those who dream of making an impact in life. Yes I write to you, and me. I was blessed through the very words you are going to read in this book. They gave me a new perspective in life that has increased my productivity and my zeal for life. If you take this journey and decide that you want to become the change you want to see around you, then welcome to: The Power of Methods." - by bestselling author: Servaas Steenkamp

Chapter 1
The First Chapter

The Power of Methods

A Dream Forgotten

The Power of Methods

A Dream Forgotten

Well what can I say, the dream I had was long forgotten. When I was a child I thought as a child and even, dare I say it, spoke like one. My dreams started when I was young but soon died because of life issues as it became hard. My journey was a roller coaster ride. All I remember is small snippets of the past, but enough to construct a comprehensive analysis of my childhood. I remember that we use to live somewhere in the middle of nowhere called Sannieshof, a small farming town situated in the North West Province in South Africa. That town was so small that it took a five year old boy ten minutes to walk from one end of the town to the other. I can never really remember my past as I believe that I have short term memory loss, but I know that is just an excuse. I don't remember my real father only my step dad whom my mother married when I was about seven years old.

The Power of Methods

From getting married we moved to the heart of Johannesburg. Oh how I thank God for the move. I can not picture myself living on a farm. I need the fast the fast life. I need a buzz ringing in my ears at the end of the day. I have become accustomed to the city life.

  Later, not so long after we moved to Johannesburg, my step dad retired. We then moved to a suburb called Turffontein, just south of Johannesburg. There is where I starting thinking. Meaning that I was starting to get to an age where I consciously started remembering things. I remember that my step father became extremely ill and then passed on. I remember giving my mother attitude for days. I remember being this rebellious young teen that all he wanted to do is skate. I did not have a future I looked forward to. It was utter darkness where I was. My only real escape to this horrific world was rap music. I was a very angry son. Shortly after my step father passed on I starting skateboarding. I loved it. It was like a drug to me. The adrenaline rush I experienced from jumping off of tall places no words could express. It became my obsession. I have this natural addictive nature where I can really get stuck into a topic if my heart desires to. Because skating was the only thing I knew that helped me have passion for life, I kept on skating.

The Power of Methods

My Life Changing Decision

The Power of Methods

My Life Changing Decision

I needed to earn more money to support my wife and children is what I believed. I first starting working for a ice cream shop selling ice cream for a living. I was earning a lot more there than what I was earning at the church. Inside of me I craved more. The salary wasn't enough, the hours were long and hard. I was actually lazy and sometimes I still am. I like to find the easy way of doing things. From the ice cream shop for whom I worked only six months, I moved to City Power. There I was auditing the city of Johannesburg's electric meters. With this position I was getting physically drained. I would start being more tired during the day. Imaging starting to walk from seven o'clock in the morning, to walk and then carried on walking till four o'clock in the afternoon. It was hectic hey. I was also there for six months only. Then from there I moved

The Power of Methods

to a bank. There I spent three years of my life learning the corporate world. Going from paycheck to paycheck in this fast paced world. Where one cannot afford, or so I believed, to follow one's passion and dreams.

Now as I am writing this book, I am an insurance sales person. I started this new position in January twenty eighteen. As I am writing this book I don't claim perfect success, but what I do promise is this: if these principles are followed, it will change your life for the better. As I am living this life I have seen the reason why my salary has only but doubled ever since I left working for the church. It's not because of the job I was in, it is rather the method at which I execute my passion.

The Epiphany Moment

The Epiphany Moment

If it wasn't for skating I think I would've not been here by now. Even I think that I would have not even have been able to write this book and touch so many lives as I am doing. Skating is what took me away from the music that made me depressed. It gave me a purpose. To become the next best skater in the world. I am not bragging but I do believe that if I carried on with the sport, I would have made it. Skating is what led me to meet a guy called Shane. He invited me and my best friend to a youth event where I discovered Jesus. My life was never the same again. Now skating served no purpose to me anymore. Now a journey into the Bible started. I became addicted to the Bible and learned what my true purpose in life is. I also started learning how to play guitar, a talent hidden from me. I was in grade eleven by this time. I was learning to become like Christ through my awesome

The Power of Methods

Pastor, Pastor Gavin Enslin. Senior Pastor of The Active Church. This is the place where I grew up from birth to adulthood. I say birth because I believe that I wasn't alive until I met Jesus.

The Bible speaks about being born again to enter the Kingdom of Light. So the term makes sense to me. Straight after I matriculated in two thousand and seven, I began working work my church. I was serving there for no payment. I worked there a total of a year before I started earning money there. I did everything from sound engineering to stage setups, lights, camera, drama, piano, drums, bass guitar, electric guitar and the list just goes on. I can do almost everything in the church. I worked at the church from two thousand and eight till two thousand and fourteen. I left only because I was getting married and my first child was on her way.

The Birth of The Power of Methods

The Birth of The Power of Methods

The reason of the title of this book is because of purpose one experiences when you do what you love and discover the way to get there. I thought that more money will give me more happiness, but it doesn't. The life changing decision I made was through a series on influential people in my life that helped me realize that if my dreams aren't there to help God's other children, then it's not a dream at all. God created us to specialize in a certain field. That made me realize that being the jack of all trades wasn't going to get me anywhere. Sure it helped me understand a lot of things but ultimately, if I can do a lot of different things, it doesn't help you in any way. So I learned that I need to focus on what I'm good at and start to love it.

The one thing I want to stress to you is this, and I tell this to my students all the time,

The Power of Methods

that I can not teach you anything. You can only learn from me. The way you learn determines the way you act upon your knowledge. It has been said that knowledge is power, but wisdom is putting knowledge into action. Where do you get wisdom from? The Bible says that wisdom comes from God alone. This is where the Power of Methods came from. I needed to realize how I came to certain places in my life. I did a self analysis in terms of methods. The way I executed my journey or passion.

Chapter 2
The First Hurdle

The Power of Methods

Before You Start

The Power of Methods

Before You Start

Yes, this might be the most crucial thing you read in this book. Before you start your journey into discovering the power of methods, you need to take a few minutes fixing your heart. There is somebody in this world that has hurt you. There is some pain you received that you didn't deserve. You were taken for granted. You were left lonely. You had things stolen from you. You were cheated on by someone you loved. All of these things come from the corruption of our flesh in this fallen world. The only defence you have against the hurt, the pain, the rejection is; forgiveness. You have to start the process of forgiveness in order to grasp the full extent of this book. Unforgiveness is like drinking poisen and expecting the other person to get hurt. If you keep those things that hurt you within your heart and do not forgive, you are like a person who drills a hole in their boat on the ocean and expects the boat not to sink. I personally have

The Power of Methods

received my forgiveness from Jesus which actually enables me to forgive others. Without knowing you have been forgiven, it's is difficult to forgive those that have caused extreme pain in your life.

Progress in life starts with forgiveness. I didn't forgive people perfectly in the past but I do my best to and that I try to forgive them more than I have previously. I have many faults and I pray that the people I have hurt will forgive me. As a married man, what I have learned over the years is that,the easiest and the most hurt you will cause, is in the relationship that we call marriage. There is no marriage on earth that doesn't have some problems. The one thing I learn consistently on a daily basis is that the number one thing that you need to do is to forgive people everyday. So take these skills you are about to learn, forgive those who have hurt you and get married to your purpose and see what will happen in your life. I'm not saying that what those people have done is alright, but sometimes we need to let go and let God. Some things are beyond our control and if we allow those things to stop us, then we will never achieve all that we have been created to achieve in this life. I wish you all the best and I pray you forgive those who have hurt you. Keep strong and keep pushing. You are on the right track and even if no one appreciates what you are sacrificing, they will in the end come to a knowledge of how much you have done. Keep reading and I hope this book blesses you abundantly.

# The M In Methods

The Power of Methods

The M In Methods

The M in Methods stand for Mechanism.

In every business that runs successfully you need a mechanism or vehicle that runs the business. This is what drives the business. It could be your sales department. Only you will be able to figure out which department it is in your business. This mechanism takes you from A to B. Let's take the scenario of you driving to your work everyday in your car. First things first, you have to understand that, you need to get to work in order to earn your salary. Logic dictates that if you don't go to work, then it could possibly land you up into trouble with your boss and or even eventually, you could loose your job. Does that sound right? Yes it does. Let's for a minute imagine this scenario and put ourselves in the shoes of this employee traveling to work everyday. So picture you are this employee. Your company is quite a distance away from where you stay

The Power of Methods

and to walk there is not an option. So logically a motor vehicle is needed, right? Or atleast some form of transport, correct? The motor vehicle is the mechanism used to get you from A to B, where A is your house and B is your work place. In business there is diferent ways of getting to your goal, but you have to use the right mechanism to get there. You have to use the right form of transportation to reach your business goals. If you don't use the right mechanism, you could end up late for your work(using our above mentioned scenario) or not even getting there at all. In business you could be late for your goal or even miss it completely.

    There are more factors involved in this chapter that deals with the mechanism and we will discuss them a little later. Getting to your goals is why I wrote this book. Some aspects that we will be dealing with in this book is beyond the scope of this book and more research is needed from you to complete your knowledge. I stress the fact that the consepts covered herein is very important in reaching your goals. Some of the things we will discuss on our journey will be covered in later chapters so don't be in a hurry, just take the reading of this book one chapter at a time. So keep reading. To get a better understanding of reaching that dream you have before you, is to think about what the mechanisms are in your goal. The things that transports you to you end result is the mechanism. Identify them and write them down. Without knowing how you

The Power of Methods

going to get to your goal or even what the mechanism is(that thing that will transport you to your goals), don't expect to succeed. These are the foundations of success. If you don't have the mechanism yet, that is not a problem, go and get a mechanism now. Then return and carry on reading. Don't feel bad if you don't have a mechanism or even know what it is, as long as you take the knowledge you are about to uncover and apply it. You will then come to a realization of the mechanism you need and have or identify the mechanism you need to get.

The Power of Methods

The E In Methods

The Power of Methods

The E In Methods

The E in Methods stands for Entity.

On your journey you will discover differnt entities on the road to success. These entities can be a variety of things. Let's take the example of you traveling to work. In the previous chapter you learned that you need a mechanism to get you to work, today you will learn what an entity is. I think the word is very self explainitory. An entity is basically something. So on the road to work there is different entities. Some entities are there as a stumbling block to your goal, while other entities are there to get you to your goal. An example of this concept is as follows; a bad entity to reaching your goal of getting to work is a road block. The road block is something preventing you from reaching your goal of getting to work on time. Another entity is your petrol finishing in your car. The lack of petrol will cause your mechanism of travel to cease

The Power of Methods

to move in the direction of your goal. A good entity in this scenario is a petrol station. There you will be able to fill up your tank again and reach your goal. You see, it doesn't really matter what the entity is, you will experience them. Either good or bad ones.

In your journey to reaching your goal you have to identify these entities. It is vitally important that you see them. Imagine that you didn't see your petrol tank getting empty. Imagine your mechanism never told you how low the fuel is. Imagine you never saw the road block and slowed down. If any of these entities aren't identified, dare I say it, could cause serious problems for you to reach your goal. So please make a list of the entities in your life. Later in this book you will learn how to deal with them. For now just identify them. When you identify them, you are already way more ahead than most people in this world that just live their lives never paying attention to the entities stopping them from reaching their goals. Procrastination...hint, hint, is an entity. You are a smart person so I don't need to spell it out for you. How do I know you are smart you ask? Well, you picked up this book to read, duh! Carry on reading to discover your full potential and to reach your goals.

The T In Methods

The T In Methods

The T in Methods stands for Tack.

In the previous chapter you learned about entities. In this chapter you will learn about the tack you will use to overcome those entities. This isn't a list of situations and the answers to them. There isn't a book large enough to cover all those diversified topics, rather, this chapter will teach you how to think in a sense. Tack is basically a short word for the word tactics. Now that I have mentioned the word tactics you should be thinking, planning. Without planning, how do you strategize? You can't. Most people don't plan their success. Without this crucial step in the journey, you will not reach your goal. Let's go back to the driving to work scenario. What do you do when you normally drive to work and you see a road block? If you have planned beforehand, you would normally take the next offramp. Seeing as you are on the highway to

The Power of Methods

work and you can't afford to get stuck in traffic for the next two hours. Those who are prepared normally take the next offramp and their GPS device recalculates another way of getting to their destination.

What do you do before you leave the house? Don't you check whether or not you have petrol? If you see you don't have petrol, don't you then plan on going to the petrol station first before jumping on the highway? If you jump on a highway(which might not have a petrol station on the way) without petrol, then you are asking for trouble. You should not expect to get to your destination if you didn't take into account the lack of petrol in your mechanism slash car. Please check your petrol gauge before you leave the house. With other entities like road blocks you don't have control over them, but with some other entities like running out of petrol on your journey, you do. Some problems you bring upon yourself and others are beyond your control. The one's that are beyond your control, the only thing you can control with them is the way you respond. Your attitude and planning towards this stumbling block will determine whether or not you reach your goals. So please plan. I will deal with planning in a later chapter, but for now, know that you need to plan. Carry on reading for there is a lot more things to cover in the coming chapters, so prepare your mind for a journey of a lifetime.

The Power of Methods

The H In Methods

The Power of Methods

The H In Methods

The H in Methods stands for Heading.

You probably wondering, what does headings have to do with reaching your goals? Well keep on reading and I will explain. A heading is the signs you get on your journey to your destination, ie your goal(s). Whenever and where ever you drive you will be bombarded with headings everywhere. The headings aren't bad, they are just signs of directions. They help you reach your goals. Imagine for a second that you take the wrong offramp on your way to work via the highway. That "stupid mistake" could cost you hours of driving and in our scenario, possibly your job. You can take the wrong offramp and recover, that isn't the issue here. The issue is getting to work on time. If you don't read the headings right and follow their guidance, you could end up without a job. Your goals could completely be messed up. So headings are very important

The Power of Methods

when it comes to reaching your destination. Think of it this way; if you have never travelled there before and don't know the road, your GPS is your friend, right? But who of you(retorical question cause you can't speak to me now) have had those, I would call it broken GPS's, that seem to take you the wrong way? I have had GPS's telling me to take the next offramp then recalculate as if I'm the problem. Meantime I listened to it's instructions as to where I need to take the next left.

Without a mechanism, this wouldn't be possible. Without entities and tactics, headings will mean nothing. Each one builds upon itself. It's like steps you follow(At least I hope you follow them) everyday. The reason why this book will help you reach your goal isn't the fact that I reveal this great mistery, but the fact that I show you that you are currently applying these methods everyday. The realization of this fact I hope hits home. If you haven't realized that you do these things by now then I will pray for you. You need to realize that you are currently successful and that you can reach any goal you want to reach. Just realize the truth about your journey and success is bound to follow you. You might not think you are successful but I beg to differ. The fact that you are reading this book has to speak to you; that you are successful or atleast have the ability to be successful. These are principles that you live by. Make a list of the different headings in your life that will take you to your destination. It could be something

The Power of Methods

your father said to you. A heading could've been something your Pastor said to you. Whatever your headings, I suggest you heed their instructions. Carry on reading for more mind blowing stuff I promiss.

The Power of Methods

The O In Methods

The Power of Methods

The O In Methods

The O in Methods stands for Order.

If you think the previous chapter was loaded, wait until your hear this. Let's look at our mechanism for a second. Our mechanism in this scenario has been a car as it takes us to our destination correct? Now as most of you guys know, if the mechanism's instructions aren't followed to the tee, then something can go horribly wrong. Let's go to driving school for a minute. When we learned about how to drive, what was one of the very first things we learned? Wasn't it clutch control? Let me say this; if the right order of clutch control isn't followed there are some things that will happen. Firstly the car will stall. Oh the dreaded stall in the driving test, instant failure. So it is with your goal. If you don't follow the right steps, don't expect to move forward and be successful. First you press the clutch pedal then you change to the right gear using the

The Power of Methods

gear lever, and so on and so on. Sounds boring doesn't it? Well, this boring step is probably the strongest step you will ever learn. If you don't start from the bottom and learn all you can when you there, don't expect to be a CEO of that company you are working for. If you don't know your job or worse, know it but do it with a half hearted attitude, don't expect to reach your goal of being a CEO. In your journey of success there is a method to follow and a road map to be led by.

If you skip anything and think that a short cut will get you there, then you might not reach your goal. Sometimes the short cut has been closed till further notice. Sometimes the short way or the quickest looking way might get you highjacked, then how will you reach your goal then? Yes you can catch a taxi, but then you riding on the success of another and worse, paying for it. Don't you want the satisfaction of making your goals a reality? Is there not something inside of you striving to stand? Making clever arguements about success doesn't get you to your goal. Having "higher arguement" will cause you to miss the headings in your life and you might take the wrong offramp. So be care full, meaning full of care. Actually care about where you are and where you are going. People who walked with you this journey deserve you to be successful. Don't let them down because of short cuts. Short cuts have double meanings. Yes its about destination but also for all the business men and woman out there. Think about this; if

The Power of Methods

you do short cuts as in labour, who is going to buy your product? Those people you employ are also your customers. Replacing them with robots don't help your cash flow. People need to be employed to earn cash to be able to go to the shop to buy your product. Think people think. There is a way of doing things and if that way isn't followed, you won't reach your goal.

I know this chapter has been a bit lengthy but I hope it has helped you. Make a list of the order needed in order for your goals to be successful. Then once you have come up with the right order of things, eg: baking a cake. You will be able to see the roadmap to success and hopefully you will execute the plan. There is no purpose in you reading this book and do nothing with this information you have educated yourself with. Please go and do something physical to reach your goals, but don't forget what you have learned so far.

The Power of Methods

The D In Methods

The Power of Methods

The O In Methods

The D in Methods stands for Disposition.

This might be the most vital piece of information your about to read. Disposition speaks about your attitude. Yes I said it. Attitude. If your attitude is not right every single day when you wake up, then you might possibly not reach your goal(s) at all. Everyday, day by day, if your attitude is not that of an olympic winner, pushing to get to their goal, your goal might be running away from you. Your first task in the morning when you wake up is to make your bed. Once completing this task you have set yourself up for success. It is a way to program your brain that even though everything has failed during the day, at least you accomplished a task. Think about our scenario that we have been speaking about earlier. If you wake up and feel like you don't want to go to work, chances are that you won't. But if your attitude says; it

The Power of Methods

doesn't matter how I feel, I will go to work, then the chances are that you will do it. Imagine you feel tired or even sick but your attitude is that which states; they will be able to do the work without me, this should scare you. If they will be able to do the work without you then you are not beyond being fired from your current position. But if your attitude states; I need to get to work cause my team needs me, this is the better attitude. For one it shows that you know your importance and secondly, it shows you know the value of team work.

Disposition isn't an easy topic to cover because it deals with a lot of things at once. It deals with your passion. It deals with your vision. It deals with your determination. It deals with your goals. It deals with your beliefs. It deals with a very extensive list of things. Things that go beyond the scope of one book. You have to go more in details and search out these different things that make up your attitude. Your mission, if you choose to accept it, is to wake up in the morning and decide what attitude you want to have. Do you want a winner attitude, or do you want a defeated attitude? The determining factors in reaching your goals is in the attitude in which you tackle your day. The bible speaks about: that you should not worry about tomorrow cause it has enough problems of its own. Instead focus on the problems of today that you can solve and solve them. Focusing on tomorrow's problems is an impossible feat as

The Power of Methods

you can not see into the future and you don't even know what your problems of tomorrow is going to be. So why worry about them. It is a wasted energy and a dream killer this thing called worry. There hasn't been any succesful person that worried themselves to success. Worry is the wrong attitude to have. Do you see how all of these things interchange and that you can't do one without the other? Everything walks hand in hand and if one part fails, every part fails.

It has been said that a team is only as strong as it's weakest link. It's the same as; you could own the fastest car in the world, but you will only be able to drive at the speed of the car in front of you. This means basically that if whoever you are following isn't going at the pace you are going at, then you need to find someone else to follow. It could also mean that you are suppose to be the leader in that field, work place etc. If you find yourself traveling at break neck speeds but having to slow down on the highway because of someone else's lack of speed, you might need to consider overtaking them and become the leader.

The Power of Methods

The S In Methods

The Power of Methods

The S In Methods

The S in Methods stands for System.

What is so special about the S in Methods? Why a system you my ask? A system combines all we have learned and helps us to stay focused and on track. Because you have purchased this book, you have been given a special discount to the following products namely: The TALK program & implementation of The Power of Methods in your business. But that's not all; you also get, as an added bonus that we will include, a leadership program called NURTURE. This is where your leaders and those in authority in your company will learn to understand the dynamics of their team. We will also be teaching new leaders the skills they will need to create that dream team you have been wanting but haven't been able to get. But that is not all, we will bring up the overall morale in the company through our patented rewards

The Power of Methods

program. This program will help your leaders to reward their staff and get the most productivity from them as employees. So what is so special about the S in Methods? The S is the system that we are offering you here today. This system has revolutionized how business get things done from their employees with the right attitude.

Let's be blunt here, most employees don't care about the companies they work for, correct? What if there was a way to get your employees' heart on track and caring for your business as if it was their own? Wouldn't you want people to work in your company as if they were responsible for everything that happens there including the workplace atmosphere? In the next chapters of this book we will be going through the system with you in more details. If you want to radically change or upgrade the work atmosphere for your company, I suggest that you stick it out in terms of reading this book. The value in these next chapters I can't quantify for you as it has different values for different people. Not everyone is suffering from the same problems and not everyone is at this stage where you are at mentally. So keep reading and let's deal with your current situation and your current leaders.

The Power of Methods

Closing Arrangements

Closing Arrangements

In closing this chapter I would like to say something...

This has been an eventful journey and I hope that this book has been a blessing to you. Because you have stuck out this long I thought of giving you a final special offering. My previous offer that included TALK and the Leadership NURTURE program, I will now discount it even more now.

Chapter 3
What Is
TALK?

The TALK Methodology

The TALK Methodology

We have a special bonus for you namely our program called TALK. It stands for: Technical Action Learning Keys. It is a program specially designed in the implementation of the Power of Methods. It is there to help you and your business take the key learning points of this book and apply them. We will call them TALK-ing points for your business.

The Power of Methods

Building Blocks or Sandcastles?

The Power of Methods

Building Blocks or Sandcastles?

Building blocks or sand castles? What is this all about? Why building blocks? Why sand castles? All will be revealed my friends, all will be revealed. Before I go into this topic I just want us to think a bit on the concept of a building block. In your mind picture this building block and imagine what you can do with it. If you thinking of toys, great. If you thinking of construction, great. If you thinking of work, great. If you thinking of building a house, great. All of these are correct. What do you think building blocks are? Retorical question guys. Obviously I can't hear you tell me that answer, but it was a great excercise though. Building blocks are your plans and your goals. You know, what is the point of achieving something that you didn't intend on achieving? This book did not write itself even though it took me a year to write it. I am

The Power of Methods

considered a perfectionist. Nah, I am considered an obsessed man. I wanted this book to help people and I wanted it to be right. Time was spent late into the night. Early mornings. Some chapters I deleted and started over. It was all worth it. It was all part of my plan. My journey to deliver this book to you guys. Am I proud? Obviously as a man that has never written a book before, releases a best seller online. Heck I'm proud to have achieved something. This book has helped me achieve my goals and I wrote it to help you guys achieve yours. In other words, without a clear direction(which is a plan), how do you expect to reach anywhere at all. Start making plans today. Start dreaming of making plans today. Be obsessed with your dream enough to be consumed everyday of every hour of every minute of every second with it. "Servaas, I don't want to write a book", I didn't say you must write a book. Whatever you want to achieve, whether it be the new job I want to get or something completely different, plan. Set a goal to achieve that dream. Now we get into what sand castles are. Picture or imagine being on the beach as a child building those sand castles that we all love. What a nice scene of peace and beauty. What a dream. Then the terrible sea water came and wiped our sand castles out. The sadness of losing that fantasy. That dream might possibly haunt you for the rest of your life. What could've been. What should've been. The point of this story is this: sand castles are dreams with no

The Power of Methods

action. They are fairy tales and will never become real. Life's troubles(represented by the sea) comes and wipes your dreams out. Leaving you with a scar worse than anything you can possibly imagine in your worst dreams. The scar is: what is the point of building for that which I build will only be wiped out later or at the most inconvinient time. Yes, I understand you. I understand that your airy fairy dream has just died. Maybe now it is time to change your dream. You have been told your whole life to follow your dreams. I say, follow your goals. What do you want to achieve? Do you want money, happiness, family? There is nothing that you can not achieve. Yes you can achieve them. In the next chapter we will be dealing with putting action to sand. Because what is the point of knowing about your sand castle dreams and doing nothing about it? Carry on reading and apply what you are going to learn.

The Power of Methods

Putting Action To Sand

The Power of Methods

Putting Action To Sand

Now in this chapter we are speaking about taking those dreams and actually taking actions towards them. Building a business isn't going to build itself you know. Making that extra cash isn't going to make itself. Without you starting to take the building blocks and start putting them together, you won't get what you desire. The obsessions you have for a better life and possibly more money won't become your reallity unless you start. I always say that you never learn to drive a car through a book but actually have to get into the car and drive. This book is not going t o help you drive the car. This book is designed to give you the theory and understanding of the road markings, the road rules that you will need in order not to cause an accident on the road. This isn't the final steps toward your goal but rather the first. When you start this journey of taking those building blocks from the previous chapter and start incorporating them into your

The Power of Methods

everyday life, then you are starting to build. The first thing you have to do is to take action. To go. After going or taking the action you will find that maybe the dream you had isn't what you really want. Maybe making money isn't the actual goal. Maybe looking after your family is the real goal. Maybe you just wanted bragging rights? Maybe the decision you made isn't the decision that will get you on the right path. This is why the building blocks you choose are vital to building. First go and finish your blocks, then come and build. First go and get your dream, your real dream. The dream that speaks to your heart and sould and body and mind. The one thing that you have been obsessed with your whole life. Think about this. Is this dream actually a tool or a stepping stone to my actual dream? After you have gone and get then we can start to build. We can start changing those sandcastle dreams in a solid foundation from which your business or goals are formed to succeed. This is a crucial step towards your goal because if you don't cement the dream and make it a solid framework, then when the sea of life comes it will wipe it out completely. You have to build on a solid foundation. This in a sense is a soul searching phase. Who are you? What do you really want? Is what you really want good? Can I get what I want without hurting my fellow human beings? Can I giveaway this gift that I received? Is my goal a blessing or a curse? Is my goal a gift? Can I replace my goals with new ones? All these questions you

The Power of Methods

can start asking yourself and more. After all, this is your dreams we are talking about here. Not some airy fairy story of a princess from a land far away. You have to succeed. You owe it to yourself. You owe it to your kids. You owe it to your wife or husband. There isn't time to waste. You have to start working towards your dreams today. Actually you have started, by starting t o read this book. By you oppening up this book shows me that you are serious about your dreams. So let's get going to get and build. Read on.

Chapter 4
I'm an
IDIOT, really?

The IDIOT Methodology

The Power of Methods

The IDIOT Methodology

My whole life people haved called me the worst names that anyone can imagine. The worst of all these were that I'm an idiot. I didn't like that because I know my worth but couldn't express it into the reallity that seemed to govern this world. So eventually I had to make a choice. A choice that changed my life forever. The choice was that whatever negative things people might say to me, I'm going t o find a way of turing it into a positive. So the main negative thing spoken to me was that I was an idiot. So in the chapters to follow you will get to learn how a changed my negative to a positive and how that actually changed my life. It defined my new way of thinking and allowed me the stand firm in times of great tribulations. Now nobody could have the power over who I am but me. I decide who I want to be and what I stand for. Once you grasp the following concepts, I pray that you will know who you are fully or at least be on the road of

The Power of Methods

self discovery. If you don't know who you are, how do you expect that anyone else will know who you are. Just remember: this world is full of confusing messages and it will be your aim to see through the garbage and discover the diamond trapped within. Read further.

The Power of Methods

The I in IDIOT

The Power of Methods

The I in IDIOT

With the word idiot, I actually used technique commonly known as abreviation to change what this word means to me. To change the definition completely. The I in the word IDIOT stand for INTELLIGENT. So when people call me an Idiot, I think about the word itself and I agree with them. I am Intelligent. You see that the bible says: So a man thinketh, so is he. Meaning: these people aren't attacking me but themselves. They can't stand the thought that some one other than themselves are succeeding in the things they are failing at. So yes. I am Intelligent. Thank you for the compliment kind sir. I didn't realize my worth until I started seeing the world I this way. People aren't seeing your worth because they themselves can not see their own worth. So forgive them and take their feedback or complaint and turn it into a resolution. You as a company have to change your complaints into compliments. People

The Power of Methods

might not understand your goals or your vision but you should not allow them the cloud your dreams in negativity. Why give them the power over your future? Do they love you? Do they want you to succeed? So yes I am intelligent and so are you. Live it. Breath it. Be it.

The D in IDIOT

The Power of Methods

The D in IDIOT

Another piece of the puzzle is the D in the word IDIOT.. The D stands for DYNAMIC. When somebody calls me an idiot I think about the word and reply. Yes I am Dynamic. How did you know? I don't settle for average. I want to be dynamic or entertaining. Dynamic can mean so many things on so many levels to each person but to me it means: not bored or boring. My life is busy with many ups and downs. But heck what roller coaster ride would be fun if it was a straight and boring ride. The reason we go on roller coasters is because of the thrill of the ups and the downs. Don't let life get you down because there is ups and there is downs. Cherish your moments on the ups and learn from your downs. Remember that if you have hit rock bottom it just means you have found a foundation to launch yourself with. Rocks are hard but you can't go any lower. So logically the only way is up. So if you down know that the ups are next, so lift up

The Power of Methods
your head. Be ready. Be dynamic.

The Power of Methods

The Second I in IDIOT

The Power of Methods

The Second I in IDIOT

The second I in the word IDIOT stands for INFORMED. So when somebody comes to me and says that I'm an IDIOT I respond: how did you know I'm INFORMED? Informed to means I know my stuff. I know my craft. I am up to date with the latest development in my area where my dreams have led me. Staying informed is a choice. It doesn't take talent but rather a decision. You have to make the daily choice to be first and not last. Be the one people look at to be inspired by how you are always informed. Don't wait for people to tell you what is happening but rather be the one telling people about the latest development. They might not catch on at first but carry on. They might even riducule you and say stuff like: I will never change, or stop waisting your time etc. But imagine the feeling you will have about yourselve when those who are behind you, start to catch up. They will come to you and shake your hand and say things like: how

The Power of Methods

did you know? If it wasn't for you then I would've never climbed over this hill. Remember that your positive nature shall start to help the people around you and that should be the goal.

The Power of Methods

The O in IDIOT

The Power of Methods

The O in IDIOT

The O in the word IDIOT stands for OPPORTUNIST. So when someone comes to me and says that I'm an idiot I say: How did you know I'm an opportunist? This point here speaks about being someone always looking out for opportunities. The reason for this is because there are so many opportunities passing us by everyday and if we not looking, we won't see them. There is a lot of potentials new ways of generating streams of income and if we not ready for them, then they will go to the person who is. Haven't you ever heard of these pyramid schemes where Johnny put in a hundred dollars then after 3 months received twenty thousand dollars but then as soon as you learn about this pyramid scheme, it falls flat and people now can't get their money? What if you were the one on top of the pyramid? It would've meant you received the twenty thousand dollars, isn't it? So what happened? Where were we? Were we sleeping

The Power of Methods

when this pyramid scheme came out? Yes. The opportunity went to those who were looking for it. Look, I'm not saying that pyramid schemes are a good thing. I am merely using them as a picture of our everyday reality. We are sleeping and we miss out. So yes I am an opportunist.

The Power of Methods

The T in IDIOT

The Power of Methods

The T in IDIOT

The T in IDIOT stand for TENACIOUS. So when somebody calls me an IDIOT I say: how did you know I'm TENACIOUS? I hold on to things like a pitbull. I carry on carrying on with that thing wich entangles my mind at that current moment. I am obsessed with what I'm doing. I am crazy passionate about what I do all the time. People can not understand me. Yes, I am tenacious. I keep a firm hold on the things that matter. If you are to be known throughout your life, let it be because you have had a firm grip on the things that matter. Some might look at you funny but their lives are falling apart and they don't know it yet. When ever you decide to go for your dreams, you will need this character withing you. You will have to. The reason why I say that is because you already have had things come against you as you tried following your goals. Already before you started reading this book you have encountered problems. You were

The Power of Methods

searching for an answer to your problems, that is why you picked up this book to read. I can't blame you. If this book was written by someone else I would've also picked it up because the goal is greater than pain experienced and the book worth more than the money spent to buy it. I'm not saying that after reading this book that all your problems will go away, but actually that they might even increase. The reason for this is because you ahve expanded your mind and maybe even aimed a little higher this time, so logically, the trouble will increase. I know that having the IDIOT mentallity might be strange for some people, but my prayer and hope is that this will be an example of what you can do in your life. By taking a negative and turning it into a positive way of going forward to reach your goals. Idiot is my word, maybe some other word affects you more than idiot does. I encourage you to find that word that kills you on the inside, write it down, go to a dictionary and try to find words that start with the letters of that word that you would like to be known as. Write them out. This excercise is called the acronymn excercise. You can do this, after all: your an IDIOT, Intelligent Dynamic Informed an Opportunist and Tenacious. Every one of these words can define who you are. Maybe you are more informed than others. Maybe you are more of an opportunist than others. It doesn't matter, just be who you are meant to be. Now read further.

Chapter 5
Your Crash Course To The Methods Methodology

The Methods Methodology

The Power of Methods

The Methods Methodology

Method in: achievement of goals through action.

**Mechanism (machine device)
Entity (object that exist)
Tack (course of movement)
Heading (title)
Order (arrangement organization)
Disposition (personal temperament)**

Mechanism = what machine are you using to achieve your goals example : you use your car (Mechanism) to get to work (goal) likewise we all have a mechanism that we use to get to our goals.

Entity = in your quest to achieve there will be entities that get in your way and there will be objects you encounter during your trip that will

The Power of Methods

help you in your journey to success.
Example : on your way to work you might run out off fuel and need to stop by a gas station likewise we all need to make sure of what entities we bump into or what entities we try to bump into.

Tack = speaks about course of movement or in a war scenario tactical advantage.
Example : when driving to work and you are running late, a tactical/Tack decision could be to change the route you are taking for a quicker route or a more dangerous way is to speed likewise we all are tempted to speed sometimes specially when you driving behind a granny.

Heading = whenever you encounter a heading in your method either we tend to stop and read it or we ignore it. Maybe we have seen the heading before and have become numb to its affects maybe it's the heading in the newspaper.
Example : on the highway if you miss the off ramp heading you could find yourself going down to Durban instead of Sandton likewise we all have to read the headings place before us to warm us off potential dangers and to let us know where to get off.

Order = we do things in a particular order to make certain things work.
Example : if you change the gear before you push in the clutch pedle, we will all know

The Power of Methods

whats going to happen in that scenario! Likewise we all have to follow a certain order of doing things that allow our mechanism to work.

Disposition = personal temperament is the last and most important part of your journey, like someone once said attitude equals altitude. You can have the fastest car but have the attitude of a granny you will only go as far and fast as your Disposition.

Chapter 6
The Second Hurdle

What Is NURTURE Leadership?

The Power of Methods

What Is NURTURE Leadership?

Over the years I have worked for many companies and have seen many different ways how those companies treat their employees. Some good, some bad but I haven't really seen what I'm going to explain to you guys next. This is something I would love to see in every company all over the world but I mean like every company. If what is to follow becomes the standard at which employees will be treated, I think that we would have a new revolution at hand where employees refuse to be fired. Where even if the company can't afford to pay them anymore, that those same employees would work there for free for the next year just to help the company get back on it's feet. I'm talking about a mind shift in the employment rates of the world. Imagine your a boss of a company and you know your employees have your back. No matter the

The Power of Methods

situation they are there to help you build your dream business and in turn you help build theirs. That is the heart of what you are about to read next. A dream. A vision. A perspective of things to come. Adapt what is to follow and your world might possibly change for the better. Hey, if you don't like it then skip. I would encourage you to reconsider. You have liked what you have read so far in this book but what's to follow is even better I think than anything before. Keep on reading.

The N In NURTURE

The Power of Methods

The N In NURTURE

The N in NURTURE stand for Notice. When it come to development of employees the principle of noticing them applies. There is nobody on this planet that doesn't want to be noticed by their authority especially those who want to succeed. Those that want a raise and those who seek a better position or career aim to be seen by those people who make decisions. Those of which are in charge. On a side note, those that don't seek attention blatently seek approval without many words spoken. They are the introverts so to say. They want to be noticed for all the small things they contribute to the company. When you as an employer notice your people, you have already started the nurturing process. The nurturing process is all about growing your people. It's about healing. It's about changing people's perceptions that companies only see them as a number. I love family business' because it isn't really about the numbers but about grooming

The Power of Methods

the son or daughter to take over the company one day. So the Father or Mother grooms or should I say, nurtures their child to lead in the business. If every company took on this idea and started nurturing their staff to be leaders, then the sky is the limit. Aren't you tired of late coming employees that blame traffic every single day? Aren't you tired of explaining the same thing every single day and hoping that your employee(s) can catch the vision? Knowing fully well that if they caught the vision that they(the employees) would run like the wind and achieve great things for the company. Well, it starts with the nurturing process. It starts with you noticing your employee. Seeing them in the light as a son or daughter might be hard but I want to encourage you by reminding you that that employee is just a human like you. They have dreams, wishes, wants, needs and much more. They need your support as much as you need theirs. See your employees more like partners than workers. See them as the greatest resource you have. If firing one of your employees doesn't cause pain in your heart, then you don't respect them enough as people and partners helping you achieve your dream.

The U In NURTURE

The Power of Methods

The U In NURTURE

The U in NURTURE stands for Understand. When it comes to growing yourself and growing your people, it is a vital step to achieving that goal. The understanding you have of your people will lead you to the treating of them. Let me give you an example of a reality I see everywhere I go. There has not been a company so far in my experience that have gotten this right. The reason for, the example that is about to follow, this is because companies only see their employees as an asset and a nubmber instead of seeing them as human. Think about this: The pregnant woman that is about to give birth. She gets, here in South Africa, only three months to spend with her baby as paid maternity leave. This example is only for most big corporates, this is not talking about the companies that don't even give maternity leave at all(and there is a lot of them). For most part the big corporates give the three months paid

The Power of Methods

maternity leave and if you want more months you have to apply for non paid leave. And in most cases these non paid leave requests get declined because of business needs. What about the baby's needs? What about the mother's need to recover from the c-section? What about the father's need to spend some time with his kid? Most often than not the father gets declined. And once you start pushing the corporate to be more leanient towards this outcome, they start threatening your job and career. This all has to stop if you want to grow your people. In Canada they maternity leave is paid for a year and the father too. This is why strong families are build. Strong family structures equals to strong economic conditions. People love Canada. People rave about the working conditions there and the benefits. Think about what I am sharing with you today. So in other words, grow your people, grow your topline. Enough said. Read further.

The Power of Methods

The R In NURTURE

The Power of Methods

The R In NURTURE

The R in NURTURE stands for Relate. The only way to grow is to relate. How can a Billionaire teach about achieving his financial success if he inherited his or her wealth? They can not because they have nothing to relate with when it comes to poor people. The only people they can talk to is the wealthy kids of today. When a leader of any organization leads with relation to those of which he or she is relating to, they become more effective in their development of their people. To nurture or to grow somebody in your orginization is the key ingredient to success. A CEO once said when someone asked him asked him regarding growing his people, is he not scared they are going to leave? He replied with, would it not be more scary for an orginization that someone stays in the company for fifteen years without growth? The point is this. Grow your people and learn to understand and relate to them. To their needs and wants. Relating is probably th

The Power of Methods

hardest thing to achieve cause we all come from diverse backgrounds and cultures but I can assure you of this, from my years of doing sales, there is something you can relate to with that person. Whether it be their families, their wives, husbands, kids, an experience like traffic going to work, driving, food. I would call these universal experiences. Everybody goes through the same kind of things on a daily basis. Maybe they don't like their current manager cause they feel like that guy keeps on talking down on them like they some kind of piece of meat. Maybe the hate taking a taxi to work because the taxies is not a very convenient way of traveling to work. Maybe you can even relate to a broken or successful relationship they might be experiencing right now. The list is endless. The crux of the matter is; spend the time needed to learn how to relate to your people. There is something happening in schools these days where some teachers are going the extra mile to create their own unique handshakes with every child making them feel special and loved which in turn caused the learners to excel in their school work. This is a big issue that needs to be handled. So go and handle it. Carry on reading.

The Power of Methods

The T In NURTURE

The Power of Methods

The T In NURTURE

The T in NURTURE stands for Trust. One of the biggest problems we face these days are the lack of trust that we can issue as a company to our staff and rightfully so. Many a staff have stolen from their companies and deserve not to be trusted. People think coming to work late is okay and that it does not effect the business, but I would like to say that that is called stealing. If you keep on stealing, don't you think eventually you'll be caught? Won't you go to jail for stealing? We actually have a culture of thieves prowling around seeking from whom they can devour. This is unacceptable people. I want everybody to think about this: those who steal, make it hard for the rest of us who want to make an honest living. The companies clamp down on their policies and procedures to prevent theft which in turn make the job descriptions more complex and in turn cause unemployment to raise up. Don't you guys see how everything is

The Power of Methods

connected? When crime goes down, jobs become more and vice versa. Think about it. When its hard to get a job to provide for your family, the temptation is there to go into illigal actions like stealing, dealing drugs and so on and so forth. I want you guys to wake up to the reality that the more jobs are in the market for people to attain without having a list of requirments, the more crime will decrease. Now I'm not saying you as a company must drop your standards, do not hear what I'm not saying. What I mean is: grow your people. Train them in the roles you need them in. Don't ask for an MBA in Business if the job can be done by someone trained on the job and experience is keyd in. In the corporate world someone that has a wife and kids is seen as a more reliable employee as that person is there to provide for his family and isn't there to mess around. With that said, if a company is always looking for fresh blood to employ it kinda acts like a tool to help the current employees to stay on their top performance slash game. Trust is earned and can not be given. If you guys, employee and employer, can work out your trust relationship, then the sky is the limit. Read on.

The Second U In
NURTURE

The Power of Methods

The Second U In NURTURE

The second U in NURTURE stands for United. This one is a tricky subject because it is easy to be devided when you have different visions in the relationship. Most employees haven't even read the vision and mission statement of the company. And likewise many companies haven't taught their vision to the employee or even bothered asking their employees what their visions are for the future. Does this sound right? Big corporates believe HR has handled this in the interview stage, but I would like to propose that even thought HR asked the person; where do you see yourself in the next ten years, that that employee or potential employee lied just to get the job. A friend of mine Grant Cardone(best selling Author, King of Sales, And Guru. #enoughsaid) had this crazy idea to make a television show where he interviewed he's

The Power of Methods

potential employees together in a room and through a series of tests. It's almost like they went through a gauntlet as gladiators and where only the strong survived. If we look at old school Chinese movies about a student and his master teaching him Kung-Fu, we learn that the master(employer) put the student(employee) through various of tests to improve(nurture, grow) him. If he failed the test he would have had to retry until he succeeded. Lots of people try, fail and then give up. I propose that you should try, fail, get up, try, fail, get up, try, fail, get up until you succeed. No great person gave up. Now you probably wondering; what has all of this to do with the topic at hand called unity. We'll I'm happy you asked. How can one be expected to know your company's vision without preaching to your employees and vice versa, how can the company know your vision as a person if your too scared to loose your job because you have conflicting interests. It's okay to have a different view. With that said, remember that you are not their to work for yourself but rather for someone else, so suck it up and work like your life depended on it. Become united where you are and you will see progress. Maybe you will start even liking your job. Carry on reading.

The Second R In
NURTURE

The Power of Methods

The Second R In NURTURE

The second R in NURTURE stands for Respect. Every person on this planet deserves respect in some shape or form. Some people demand more respect while others cling to the very little respect they get. Irrespective of all of these factors, you as a business owner needs to be un-bias. You have to respect all people the same. It has nothing to do with their skin colour or the colour of their hair. It even has nothing to do whether or not they are a male or female. It has nothing to do with whether they were born in a poor family or a rich one. What most people do is judge a person from their background like they had a choice where they were born. This is the beginning of the end if these sorts of thoughts come to you. The thoughts of gender inequality, racial tention and so on. You can not build yourself by destroying others. The

The Power of Methods

first step to respect is self respect. You can not respect people when you have no self respect. If you don't love yourself first then you can not possibly expect yourself to love anybody else, could you? Where there is an overflow of goodness in your heart towards your fellow humans, to nurture them, care for their needs, to strengthen their minds and so forth, will come the nurturing of those under your care. The question asked is: what if I groom them then they leave me as an employer? The real question should be rather: what if I don't groom then, then they leave me as an employer? You see, there is only really two choices here. You can not be sitting on the fence with this one. You either respect people, or you don't. Respect is earned you say? Let me propose a new philoshophy, give and you will receive. Sow the goodness of respect and then you will reap the harvest of respect. Show respect through your actions and words. The ultimate life to be lived is that of respect. Imagine no one respected your business? Would they buy from you? Would they even enter your store? There is some form of respect when it comes to the sales process that allows a salesman to close a deal. There is no salesman that can close a deal without the buyer respecting the salesman. Build rapport with your client through the respect you give. Don't give lip service, rather get your heart and mind to a position where you respect people irrespective of what they have done. Be the giver because those people you battle to

The Power of Methods

respect, you have no control over. The only control you have is the way you respond. The choice is yours but I urge you to choose respect as the first thought. Read on.

The E In NURTURE

The E In NURTURE

The E in NURTURE stands for Encourage. Its easy to be the non-encourager. Its easy to pull your people down through insults and demeanor. Think of the word: de-mean-or. It means: outward behaviour or bearing. Meaning basically that; the way you are expressive through the way you walk, talk, listen and speak. I always look at this word in a different way. You can either be de-mean-or de-kind-er. It's your choice. I personally have done both in different scenarios. It's not that you will get this right all the time but you aim to direct kindness at people. Let your goal be kindness. Kindness is something that goes beyond the way you react to situations. Kindness actually seeks out to whom he or she can be a blessing today. You see, people mistake patience as kindness but this is a mistake. To have patience is to have the right attitude to something which has happened to you. To be kind is to have the right action

The Power of Methods

towards someone who doesn't necessary deserve your kindness. For example: that guy who is begging you for money on the side of the road who hasn't contributed anything to society but potentially have contributed to the crime in the area, to give him something like money is to show kindness. I hear you. People like those druggies shouldn't be helped cause we aren't helping them get out of their situation by giving them money. I hear you. If we give them money we are destroying them cause now they have the means to go and drink that money away. I hear you. But let me make this statement: is that showing kindness? When we rationalize why we don't give? The choice is yours. Even if they don't deserve it, it's true. They don't deserve any money from us, but is this a kind attitude? Now let's bring it to your business. That worker that is always late, you know which one that is. How would you show him kindness? Is it to fire him cause clearly this job isn't for him? Or is there a better and more loving way to lead him or her on the right path? Is kindness being encouraging? Is the way to encourage your workers through kindness? Do you know the struggle of your employees working a nine to five job? What distance does this troublesome person have to travel to get to work? What are the working conditions like? Even if you are a big corporate and this employee get's a fat pay cheque at the end of the month, is that employee satisfied? Are they encouraged? Have they reached their

The Power of Methods

dreams? There are to many dynamics in your company through your employees for you to not be encouraging! If your not encouraging them, who is? Make it your responsibility to actually lead your employees where you want them to be mentally and emotionally. Don't leave it to them. They need your leadership. Read on.

Chapter 7
What Is
Your PLAN?

The Power of Methods

What Is Your Plan?

The Power of Methods

What Is Your Plan?

We have another special bonus for you namely our program called PLAN. This program takes you through the planning stages in order to help you and your business. We will call them PLAN-ing points for your business. The PLAN program will take your planning and thinking in terms of planning to a whole new level.

The Power of Methods

The P In PLAN

The Power of Methods

The P In PLAN

The P in PLAN stands for: Plot a path. Basically this is the beginning of your planning stage. This is the goal setting stage. The pathway to your dreams and desires. Imagine you are a sailor that is sailing the seven seas, going to explore the world. You have to plot the course or path to which you will be sailing or else you and your crew could end up dead or stranded on some deserted island. This is the first step and probably one of the most important steps toward your goals and dreams. This method of planning where you see the goal as a path to success is different than just writing down a shopping list hoping to receive your blessing. This method of planning where you actually plot the path, the actual roadmap to where you need to go, will ultimately get you to your goals. Which is better, a list on the wall stating that I want to be a millionaire, I want the latest BMW, I want to have a big family versus: the way to get to

The Power of Methods

a million could be one of these following paths, then you write them out like if I sold a million products at one dollar, that would make me a millionaire. Or the way to get the latest BMW is to reach an income goal of and you list it, and to reach that goal I need to do xyz. Which one seems better? Doesn't the plotting a path seem much more achievable just simply because you have a PLAN, a roadmap to reach the goal? Yes, sometimes the plans don't work out but at least you tried and failed, got back up to try again. There is no such thing as failure, only constructive feedback as to another way that is wrong to reach your goal. The main aim of this way of doing your planning like this is also a way of visualization. What you see is what you get. Haven't you ever heard that saying before? People use this saying as a mean way of saying this is all of me and there is no more to be seen. So basically that a spade is a spade. I look at this saying in a different way. What you see, IS WHAT YOU GET! So if you can visualize what you want and push and plot and learn and never give up, then success will jump on you like a thief in the night. So start this new way of planning. There is more to come, once you understand the whole concept behind the PLAN model, then this should come natural to you. Read on.

The L In PLAN

The Power of Methods

The L In PLAN

The L in PLAN stands for: Litigate Information. This is the kicker. You can't just receive a bunch of information ie. Feedback from your current situations, without taking the time to analyze the information given to you. This is a skill lawyers have learned. They litigate information for their court cases cause it's needed for their clients. So to you have to litigate the information life throws at you. If you don't, how do you think you are going to be a match in the court room of life? Cause life will throw you a curve ball you haven't thought about. Some angle of attack that catches you of gaurd. Do you think life is your friend? Life will come at you hard and with every weapon at its disposal. The art of litigation is crucial for your planning. Without the skill to read into your life and plan, I don't know how you will be able to make it. You have to learn to interpret what life is saying to you. You have to read the signs. Litigation is almost the

The Power of Methods

discipline of studying the information. Now you might be thinking, I hate studying. Me too, but I love to learn. Its a different attitude all together. So the second step in this planning procedure after plotting, is litigation. Study the information you have just plotted and ask yourself this question; is this the right course of action? Will this course of action get me into the promised land? Can I succeed with this plan? Is this me? Who am I? Remember that these teachings are all about your pholosophy and approach to a new thinking of planning. What I would really like you to do is to learn to understand the concept because once you understand you will never have to open this book again after reading it. Understanding the information is the key to open up many doors in your life. First understanding needs to come. Push to understand. Make it your life goal to understand everything. So by doing this you will be forced to expand your mind to a world of possibility. There is more to life than just what you see. But understand will get you into another, dare I say it, universe. Read on.

The Power of Methods

The A In PLAN

The Power of Methods

The A In PLAN

The A in PLAN stands for: Actuate Yourself. Its all good and well that you have plotted the best path and you have litigated all aspects of your plan to see every turn. But without the use of this powerful tool called self motivation(actuate yourself), there is no way to follow your own plan. How many people decide and plan to go to the gym every new year but fail because they lack the self motivation to carry on when the pain starts getting real. The term we can use here is also determination. Determination to succeed. It is also sometimes refered to the fight or flight symtom. Its also called: do or die. This is one of the most important factors to your success and reaching your goals. There are so many people in this world that can testify to this simple fact of determination and perseverance that I don't need to say much. You have to start motivating yourself in everything. You can not allow any negative thoughts or speech

The Power of Methods

to surround you where you are. Get rid of those negative people in your mind. Stop talking to yourself. Start embracing change and growth. Silence those internal voices that growd out the real you. Make it loud and clear that you are a sober minded person and everything is clear to you. You might not have understanding now but you will get it once you pursue it. Keep on pushing and dreaming good dreams. Choose the right things to leave your concience clear of any rotten thing. Even though you don't think that those things affect you, it does. Esspecially when self actuation needs to happen. Every gossip session you attend with negative people gets stored in your subcontious mind and that does affect you. This hard drive called your brain records everything and esspecially every small detail. What is happening internally will come out externally. What you think will reflect in your actions. You can't hide forever. Sooner or late you will be exposed of the secrets you keep. Those secrets keep you in bondage. Now you might be saying; I'm not keeping any secrets. I would strongly dissagree as everytime you had a bad thought of someone or any unforgiveness, that is a secret. I'm not saying you must go and confess your sins, but what I'm saying is that doing the confession will bring in inner peace. This inner peace will allow you to mute the noize around you and enable you to focus on actuating yourself. Read on.

The Power of Methods

The N In PLAN

The Power of Methods

The N In PLAN

The N in PLAN stands for: Network Market. Contrary to popular belief, there is no such thing as a self made millionaire. I didn't make my millions by myself. I needed all of you guys to purchase my book to get me closer to my goals. I needed to socialize and network with like minded people. You guys are like minded people and the reason I can say that is, obviously, you bought my book. Only those on the same path will be drawn together in the end. You chose this book because you think like me. Period. Maybe you think that I'm just saying this, no, I truly believe that we are the same in spirit and mind. We are pushing to the end. We want to succeed. We need to succeed. There is no other options for us. That plan must work. We need to make it work. We need the support to achieve our dreams. We need each other. So forget about achieving all by yourself. Don't listen to these so called self-made people, they are lying. If you look at

The Power of Methods

some of the best public speakers in the world, they can't have been so effective without their team behind them. Even the pastors have a whole team running the church service with him or her. Without unity their is no conquest. We not about winning, we are about dominating. Without our network we have no networth. We need the market just as much as the market needs us. The shop needs you to buy in order for their doors to stay open and you need their doors to stay open because you need what they are selling ie bread and milk and eggs and vegies etc. Do you see the grand scheme of things? This whole get rid of the worker in the factory nonsense will bankrupt the country. Think about this: you fire all your staff and replace them with robots that never eat, sleep or complain. Great. Productivity is at its best. The Company seems to be producing more, forgetting about their clients. What do you mean you ask? I'll explain. Those same people sitting without work or an income now can't go to the shops to buy as they have no money. Now sales of the company stops causing production to stop and in turn causes the company to shut down. So they might have saved in the short term but in the long term they actually destroyed themselves. This is all about the market. The human network market. It's best you learn this lesson fast before its too late for you. Read on.

The Power of Methods

Closing Arrangements

Closing Arrangements

You see that to PLAN has many steps and those steps require some attention to details. At least now you understand the PLAN METHOD that I apply in all my work. I hope this has blessed you and I hope above all that you understand the importance of planning. Remember to plot that path and then litigate the information whilst you are actuating yourself and network marketing. This is a journey. Success is a destination. Get there. Don't be left behind. Your life depends on it!

Chapter 8
What Does It Mean To Be Human?

The Power of Methods

What Does It Mean To Be HUMAN?

What Does It Mean To Be HUMAN?

What does it mean to be HUMAN? Have you ever contemplated this question? What differentiates us from the animals? What is the core difference about us that shows we are not animals? What is a Soul? What is a Will and Mind? What makes us tick? What drives us to be who we are? Are we but a random accident from a cosmic explosion? No we are not! We are far more than an accident and in the following chapters I will break the word HUMAN up into a way that hopefully will make us understand each other better. Read On.

The Power of Methods

The H In HUMAN

The Power of Methods

The H In HUMAN

The H in HUMAN is for HOPE. This chapter of the word HUMAN is basically going to address the way we should treat people in my oppinion or the way we lead them. People out in this world is bombarded with negative messages after negative messages and where we as employers don't need to add to their stress. So in other words, we need to give them hope. When I was working for a very big company some time ago my manager basically told me that because of my skin I am not going to progress any further in my carreer in this company. He said it in a nice way after complimenting me on my hard work I have been giving to the company. I tried to go the extra mile all the time and was probably the only serious worker there compared to my co-workers(in my own opinion) and thus this news that was presented to me crushed me. I lost all hope working for this company. I stopped being the extra mile guy. I stopped

The Power of Methods

coming to work earlier than required. I stopped staying longer after work to help my co-workers out. I stopped having a drive of passion to even be in this company. I noticed a change in me. Everybody else noticed a change in me. What was that change? Hope. I no longer had the hope that I as a father could achieve the goal of increasing my household's financial situation and hence give my kids what they deserved. You see, this crushing of a man's spirit is like poison to his bones. Obviously I can't speak about how a lady would react to a situation like this as I am not a lady. I only speak from my point of view and I hope you would be able to translate this into your own life. This lack of hope stops you from waking up early in the morning with a go getter attitude. This lack of hope destroys your self esteem and image and has the worst kind of hangover. The headaches that followed and the endless nights without sleep drove me insane. I had to escape. I had to get out of this painful situation. I started looking for opportunities to leave. Finding every excuse under the sun as to why working for this company is toxic. I didn't hate my work before, now it seemed like I hated everything about this company. I was lost. When hope is lost, the Bible calls that a sick heart. I was sick. I had a sick heart and the pain drove me to a mental instability. The lesson I learned in that time was that people need hope to come to work everyday. They need the hope of growth, stability, love and need. Without

The Power of Methods

people feeling involved, then why should they be there? Read on.

The Power of Methods

The U In HUMAN

The U In HUMAN

The U in HUMAN is for Use in the right place. Besides not having hope, one of the killers are also to do with, where a person is being used in the company. I believe in hard work as a standard to live by so naturally I tend to want to be in a situation of power. This need to be in control stems from the idea that when you are in power, you will get things done. In that big corporate where I worked for three years only, I believed that the position of team leader skipped me even though I was the most suited for the position. I learned about "friendship" when a new leader was picked. It wasn't about who is the best and would do the work hundred and twenty percent, but rather about who the leadership liked. This is a typical example of what is happening in our society where people aren't being used in the right places because whoever is in the power seat deems their friends above other human beings even though they know that their friend

The Power of Methods

is the worst person for the job. That was a mouth full. The fact that this is happening is the reason why there is political corruption in all companies. You see, as a friend you owe me 'cause if I was you, I would have helped you out. This is the mentality. Now you feel under pressure to help this "friend" out because, if they received the same power as what you just received, they would've helped you out. This I call: emotional blackmail. You pinning a fiction upon your so called friend that they should by all means "help a brother/sister out!". If you were really a good friend you would be happy that your friend is succeeding irrespective of the fact that they might "forget" about you. Yes it's hard to praise someone you helped succeed especially when they don't even acknowledge you for the help you provided. This attitude of self entitlement is a poisonous emotion that will destroy you internally. This emotion stems from the heart where a human wasn't used in the right place according to their goals, ambitions, talents and heart. Ultimately, this topic I am discussing here is a difficult internal political issue. If you want your business to grow, use people right and stop "doing favours" because those favours are toxic and can cause your company to fail. Read on.

The Power of Methods

The M In HUMAN

The Power of Methods

The M In HUMAN

The M in HUMAN is for Motive to move. Besides hope and using people in the right place(which is difficult to achieve but achievable), we now start looking at people's motives. What causes people to move. What makes someone self motivated? Is it their up bringing? What causes you to be motivated? There is an aray of different reason as to the motivation of people and calls for a book in of itself to deal with this topic. I am going to give some ideas as to what causes this "motivation". Some people are purely money driven, some of you guys are thinking. Really? A lot of people labeled me as someone who is purely money driven and even started calling me names. Which is ok. They don't understand why I do what I do and speak the way I speak. They don't understand my pain and or my passions. They quote on quote, don't see my heart, end quote. I speak about money cause it's necessary. Money solves problem like my

The Power of Methods

children's education, food on the dinner table, petrol for our cars and the list goes on. You see, money isn't my obsession, supporting my family is. Making sure my household has no insufficient needs. I came from a background where we had a lack of real food. What I mean by that is, my staple diet was dry bread with no butter or jam or anything. Just dry bread. I hate dry bread. I need butter. You see that this is my motive to move in the right direction. What is your motive to move. I want you to think about it carefully. What is in your core value system that motivates you to get out of bed every morning. What makes the sun rise for you everyday? What makes the coffee taste sweet in the morning for you? What can you say you are proud of in your life? What is your purpose? You see that all people or should I say humans have the necessary need of motivation. Motivation helps us achieve our dreams. Motivation helps us to be humans. We are not monkeys that live on instinct fighting for food everyday. Life is so much more than food or the clothes we wear. Find your motive to move and start moving into your destiny. I can't help you with this unfortunately. This is an internal journey of self discovery that you will need to take. Find your motivation. Some people are motivated by traveling the world. Some are motivated by health. Some are motivated to be the best and achievement. Find your story and start to complete your chapters in your book. Read on.

The Power of Methods

The A In HUMAN

The Power of Methods

The A In HUMAN

The A in HUMAN is for Assist where needed. I'm not going to repeat the previous chapters again for you, if you want, go read them again. This chapter speaks about assistance. Who doesn't need assistance? Is there really such a thing as a self made? I don't think so. The reason for this thought is because, since you left your mother's womb, you have been helped. You were taught, fed, carried and many more. The point is simply this: everything you are is an impression of someone else. Who have you allowed to influence you? In the business space, even though someone has a degree and claims theye don't need help, they do. Assistance is needed and subcontiously wanted. Nobody has "got this" really. When I first became married, I thought I knew everything about how to treat my wife, but sadly, I don't. When my first child was born, I thought I was going to be the best father in the world, but sadly, I am not. I

The Power of Methods

need assistance in everything. I learn from everybody. Even my one year old boy has taught me many things. You see, I am not "self made", but I am created. The circle you surround your self with will create you. The question is this, do you want that? Where do you need assistance? In a company setting, your staff need assistance cause they haven't got your vision. Sadly, they don't want your company to grow. They happy with what they have and are doing now. Growth is uncomfortable and many, if not all, are against it. So you do need to assist where needed in most cases. You need assistance, that is probably the reason you bought this book to read, cause you need assistance in some field where you need clarity. Does that make sense? Obviously this is a retorical question I want you to think about. The main focus of this chapter is to break the perception that you can do it on your own, you can't. Where there is a team, there is conquest. Stop trying to do everything. Start trusting people around you. I know it's hard when you are someone like me, a control freak. But in the long run it will work out. What if they drop me you ask, what If they blow your mind with their achievement? What if they do this function even better than you? Isn't that your real fear? The fear of missing out or the fear of looking small in comparison? Think about that. Read on.

The Power of Methods

The N In HUMAN

The Power of Methods

The N In HUMAN

The N in HUMAN is for Nurture Always. This is my closing chapter. This chapter is just to inform you that, you have to always be aware(especially as a leader) of how humans work. They need everything mentioned in the previous chapters plus they need what is in this chapter. In this chapter I state that all the other chapters needs to be done always. You cannot skip anything and you cannot stop doing this that you learned. You have to always keep on keeping on like they use to say. The NURTURE principles taught in earlier chapters is a need. You have to nurture your flock. How do you expect to gain wool and lamb chops out of broken and beaten down sheep? You have to take on the mantle of leadership the old shephard way when it come to leadership. Even you as a person need to reuse those steps in relation to your boss and other relationships that you value. These principles can help you in all

The Power of Methods

aspects of your life but you have to keep them close to you. Nurture the nurturing principle in your heart and do it ALWAYS! This must be who you become in order for things to change. You have to internalize these ideas and allow them to mold your character. You might say, why should I do that? My question to you is this; why not? Why did you read this book till the end then? Why did you wast your time and money? Isn't it to change something? How do you suppose anything is going to change if you are not serious? The only way to be serious is to internalize these principles in your life and live by them. Go and study the text carefully and I pray that your light inside your heart will be enlightened with understanding of how to treat people, problems and many more. I hope these philosophical METHODS will have changed some perspectives in your mind. I hope that one day I can see you too writing a book to help someone from your own experience and viewpoint of understanding. You can do it. You can help people. Just do it. Stop making excuses and just go and do something to help someone. Remember to ALWAYS NURTURE! Thank you for your time. God bless.